Work Well From Home

Staying effective in the age of remote and hybrid working

BLOOMSBURY BUSINESS

LONDON • OXFORD • NEW YORK • NEW DELHI • SYDNEY

BLOOMSBURY BUSINESS
Bloomsbury Publishing Plc
50 Bedford Square, London, WC1B 3DP, UK
29 Earlsfort Terrace, Dublin 2, Ireland

BLOOMSBURY, BLOOMSBURY BUSINESS and the Diana logo are
trademarks of Bloomsbury Publishing Plc

First published in Great Britain in 2005 by Bloomsbury Publishing Plc

This revised and updated edition published in 2023
by Bloomsbury Publishing Plc

Bloomsbury Publishing Plc does not have any control over, or responsibility
for, any third-party websites referred to or in this book. All internet addresses
given in this book were correct at the time of going to press. The author and
publisher regret any inconvenience caused if addresses have changed or sites
have ceased to exist, but can accept no responsibility for any such changes

A catalogue record for this book is available from the British Library

Library of Congress Cataloguing-in-Publication data has been applied for

ISBN: 978-1-3994-0389-4; eBook: 978-1-3994-0386-3

2 4 6 8 10 9 7 5 3 1

Text design by seagulls.net

Typeset by Deanta Global Publishing Services, Chennai, India
Printed and bound in Great Britain by CPI Group (UK) Ltd, Croydon CR0 4YY

MIX
Paper | Supporting
responsible forestry
FSC® C171272

To find out more about our authors and books visit www.bloomsbury.com
and sign up for our newsletters

Contents

Assess yourself: could you work well from home?

Working from home is an attractive option for many people, but there is a lot to think about before you rush off to equip your home office. Answer the following questions and then read on for advice on whether it's a good solution for you.

How often do you stay late at work?

a. Regularly.
b. Only if I have to meet a deadline.
c. Never.

Do you enjoy working as part of a team?

a. No; I don't like to rely on anyone else.
b. Yes, but I also enjoy working independently.
c. Yes. It means I can offload tasks on to others.

How do you plan your daily tasks?

a. I write out a schedule and stick to it.
b. I make a list of the most important tasks and hope to remember the others.
c. I tackle jobs as they come up.

What do you do when faced with many projects at once?

a. I get on with the most important ones first.
b. I choose the most interesting job and start on that.
c. I start several tasks and continue with the easiest one.

How organized is your work space?

a. Very. I know where everything is.
b. Fairly. I have been known to lose things.
c. Not at all. I don't think about the state of my desk.

How do you feel about your boss?

a. I feel that they interfere at times.
b. We have a good working relationship.
c. I rely on their guidance.

How would you describe your relationship with your colleagues?

a. Lukewarm. I keep myself to myself.
b. Good. It's professional and friendly.
c. Great. I love the camaraderie of the office.

How do you react to unexpected difficulties?

a. I'm methodical and try to deal with the problem from its source outwards.
b. I try to follow solutions to similar problems I've experienced in the past.
c. I'm not a great problem-solver and so I panic.

How would you describe the process of delegation?

a. I see it as laziness. If a job comes your way, it's up to you to deal with it.
b. It's an important process for the development of yourself and your staff.
c. It's a useful tool – if you haven't got time to do something, pass it on!

a = 1, b = 2 and c = 3.

Now add up your scores.

Everyone should read Chapter 1 first as it's full of essential questions to ask yourself about how you might adapt to a home office.

9–14: In many ways, you are ideally suited to working from home. You like to work independently and have no difficulty motivating yourself. In fact, the only problem might be that you would never switch off – you must think carefully about scheduling time for yourself. Chapter 3 will help you put some parameters around your working time. You may also have a tendency to isolate yourself from others. When you work at home, it's important to keep in touch with key colleagues and contacts; turn to Chapter 5 for advice on this topic.

15–22: You appear to have a balanced attitude to your working life and should adjust well to working from home. Don't underestimate, however, the upheaval of adjusting to a new routine; you should lay down careful foundation plans. Chapters 2 and 3 should stand you in good stead. Also, you may need some help prioritizing your tasks when you're on your own. Turn to Chapter 4 for advice on how to work out what needs doing and when.

23–27: You thrive on working with others and should think very carefully about whether you would make a smooth transition to working from home. You will have to work hard to motivate yourself and you may feel isolated. Chapters 3 and 5 will help you make the adjustment, while Chapter 6 will help you see how you can contribute to a team even if you're not in an office. Chapter 7 offers help on coping with feelings of isolation you may experience.

1
What are the pros and cons of working from home?

Since the COVID-19 pandemic, many more people work from home; some through choice, some through obligation. For many people, working from home may have been the holy grail of employment options pre-pandemic but, since that period, they have learned that it is not necessarily for them. In an ideal set-up, it frees you from the strains of commuting so that you can get your work done in peace without the many interruptions of being in an office, and still have plenty of time left to pursue other interests outside work.

However, as the lockdowns of 2020 made clear, working from home comes with other interruptions and considerations. For convenience, cost and comfort, there's nothing quite like a home office, but on the minus side, you're on your own, literally – and if you're not disciplined, you'll be spending more time with the children, the pets or in front of the fridge than working where you belong. It can take a while to settle into a routine.

If working from home is something you have never tried before as a long-term option, consider the following questions:

- Would I likely feel isolated if I'm at home more often than normal?
- Could I separate business and personal life if both were under the same roof?
- Am I a workaholic and if so, would an office at home worsen that problem?

Step one: Work out how susceptible you are to feelings of isolation

The basic fact is that some people are much more comfortable with their own company than others. Thinking about certain aspects of your personality will help you find out how suited you are to working from home on your own.

Some people are natural extroverts and thrive on the company of others. They are motivated by the attention they receive and will look to others (consciously or subconsciously) and their reactions for direction. They are naturally warm and affectionate, trusting, and believe that others are basically good. These people may be able to work effectively from home but are likely to suffer from isolation blues. They need to have a strategy to work from home and still get the contact with the 'outside world' that they need. See Chapter 7 for more information on how to cope with feelings of isolation.

More introverted people need space and time away from others to recharge their batteries as they find social interaction quite draining. They are more internally motivated and have an inner sense of mission. They may feel suspicious of others' motives and are disinclined to believe or trust them without good reason. They're also cooler and more detached in group situations. These people are more naturally suited to maintaining their balance and motivation in an isolated environment, but they too can benefit from broadening their network to get input and support from others. Turn to Chapters 5 and 6 for help on this point.

Step two: Be honest about your reasons for wanting to work at home

People choose to work from home for all sorts of reasons. There are lots of positive reasons for wanting to spend less time in the office yet still contribute to your life at work, such as growing family commitments or a decision to study part-time.

There are, however, more negative reasons that may force us to look for an escape for a few days in the week, such as:

- a difficult boss;
- office politics;
- bullying or harassment;
- an office romance gone sour;
- overwork;
- work-related stress.

Most people have suffered from one or several of these problems at one time or another, and it's worth trying to tackle the issue before seeing working at home as a way out. If you still want to work at home afterwards, fine, but think carefully about your motivations first. With a little courage and resolution, you'll feel 100 per cent better if you sort things out.

If you are unhappy at work, remember that:

✓ you have the same right as others to be treated respectfully in the workplace;

✓ you should seek help as soon as you can if you are being bullied or harassed in any way. If you feel you can't talk to your manager about this situation, tell a trusted friend, someone who works in HR or your union representative;

✓ stress can make you ill and affects not only your work life, but your home life too. It's essential that you let people know how you're feeling so that they can take steps to help you. Don't be afraid to delegate to a colleague or junior member of staff if you can; delegation isn't an admission of failure, but a sign of sensible time management;

✓ everyone makes mistakes. It's wrong to put yourself under too much pressure to be perfect, as no one else is! Remember that a mistake is only a mistake if you don't learn anything from it, so don't beat yourself up if things go awry at times. Let your manager know if you're worried about something, take steps to address it if you can, and then move on.

Working at home = workaholic?

If you know you have workaholic tendencies, think carefully about your work–life balance before you start working from home. Obviously it's important to be productive at work – it's what we get paid for, after all – but you need to be sensible about things for your own sake. Chapter 3 is full of advice on how to put a limit on your working hours, but an essential first step is being aware of your own limitations and of the need to balance the demands of work and other areas of your life.

Step three: Talk it through with those closest to you

If you have a partner, family or housemates, spending more time at home will have an impact on them too. In most cases, this will be a positive one, and in fact someone else may have suggested to you that you work more flexibly; if you have family commitments, for example, you may need to work with others to make sure babies, young children or sick relatives are looked after.

Make sure that your plans don't clash with other people's to such an extent that they make your ideas unworkable. This isn't to say that you shouldn't explore this option – for example, many couples work very successfully from home together – but just make sure that your dream scenario will work in reality.

Step four: Discuss the options with your boss

Flexible and hybrid working patterns have become the norm since the COVID-19 pandemic but it is still important to work out the best balance of days at home or in the office with your employer.

All employees, not just parents or carers, are entitled to request flexible working. There are, however, some rules. You will need to have completed six months' continuous service at the company or organization in question before making the request, you must be classified as an employee and you must not have made another request in the last 12 months.

> **TOP TIP**
>
> Remember that requesting flexible working arrangements doesn't mean that you'll automatically be granted them! You need to make a good case that stresses how your new working style will benefit the business, rather than detract from it.

You don't have to be a parent or carer to request a new working arrangement, but whatever your reasons, you have to clear it with your employer.

✔ As a first step, send your boss a short email about your plans, rather than just turning up in their office one day and firing questions at them. Unless you've had conversations on this theme before, they probably have no idea that you've been thinking about it, so a bit of advance warning will make them feel less ambushed by the whole thing.

Try to spell out why working from home, for the first time or more often, would particularly suit your role and plan in advance how you would answer the following questions:

- Do you think you will still be able to be an effective team member?

- How would a change in your working hours or location affect your colleagues?

- What will be the overall effect on the work you do, in your view?

- How could a change in your working hours affect the business positively?

If your boss agrees to your plans, first tell any colleagues or contacts who might need to know, and then you can start thinking about the logistics of setting up a home office.

Step five: Be prepared for a period of readjustment

There is a lot to think about when you're planning a new working arrangement, and setting up a home office can be a lot of fun. You have to realize, though, that there are only so many times you can come up with the world's best filing system, rehang that poster on the wall or check to see if anyone's rung you in the last five minutes. You will have to knuckle down and do some work at some point, and at first you might find it hard going.

Don't expect to be able to settle down straight away (although obviously it would be great if you can!) – it's very likely that you'll need to take some time to adjust.

Try to make, and stick to, simple to-do lists of useful tasks to help see you through the early days.

Chapters 2 and 3 will take you through the key steps to a successful home office. Good luck!

Common mistakes

✗ You don't realize how much you miss the company of others

If you're naturally a gregarious person, you may find it difficult to work away from the 'buzz' of the office.

Obviously you'd get used to your new way of working in the end, but think long and hard about whether it's the right move for you – it's just not some people's cup of tea.

✗ You decide to work from home for the wrong reasons

If you're having a difficult time at work, the idea of retreating to the comfort of your own home can be very tempting. However, it's not a good idea if there is a real and serious problem that you need to face – you'll still have to deal with it on the days you are in the office.

Remember that no one has the right to treat you unfairly in the workplace, however high up the food chain they are, and you have every right to be treated with respect. Don't stand for bullying or harassment of any kind and act quickly before your health begins to suffer.

✗ You think everyone will see it as a good idea

While working from home might be your idea of bliss, it might not suit some of the other people affected by your decision. Talk it over with your partner and/or your family to work out some scenarios that everyone's happy with, and then talk to your boss about your plans. Explain what you want to do and take care to stress how the change in your working routine will make a positive contribution to your and their lives.

BUSINESS ESSENTIALS

✓ Be sure that you're the right type of person to spend more time away from the office. Would you be happy spending more time on your own?

✓ Be honest with yourself about your reasons for wanting to work at home. Don't do it if you're trying to avoid a problem in the workplace.

✓ If you are being treated badly at work, act quickly to resolve the problem. Letting things drag on or hiding from the situation will have a serious effect on your health and happiness.

✓ If you have workaholic tendencies, think hard about whether working from home truly is a good idea for you.

At least if you're in the office you have to go home at some point!

✔ Talk through your plans with anyone who will be affected by it, such as your partner, family or housemates. Listen to any objections or suggestions they have and remember that you can't have everything your own way all the time.

✔ Clear your plans with your boss. Break news of your plans to them sensibly and give them some warning so that your request doesn't look or sound like an ultimatum.

✔ Emphasize the benefits that you working at home for some or all of the week would bring to the company.

✔ Realize you'll need a period of adjustment when you start to work from home. Set yourself sensible to-do lists so that you achieve something while you're getting used to your new set-up.

2
Setting up your home office

You may have worked from home for the odd morning or afternoon by choice or, perhaps during the pandemic you had to work at home like everybody else. In that situation, you could probably just cope with papers being spread out all over the kitchen table or pinned up on the wall of the spare room. Working like this for any length of time will, however, drive you and your family or housemates mad. If you want other people to take you seriously, you need to take a working from home set-up seriously and spend some time thinking about how it will all fit together.

Don't feel guilty for thinking through all your options thoroughly – you'll be spending a good deal of time in your home office, so it really will all be worth it.

Step one: Plan the layout of your office

When you're planning a home office, you need to think about where to locate it, how to decorate it and how to furnish it. If you're going to work from home because you've decided to start your own business, the office is even more important, as it'll be the hub of your new enterprise. Some people even make a scale drawing of the room they intend to use, then place to-scale furniture on it to decide on the best layout.

You could also take the advice of office-ware stockists – many of the larger retailers offer an office-planning service, often online.

> **TOP TIP**
>
> If you've a good eye and are handy with a computer, you could also use some software to help you plan your layout well.

First of all, think about which room in your home could best be used as, or converted into, an office. Make sure that the room you choose:

- has enough light for you to be able to work comfortably;

- has enough space for you to be able to store any relevant equipment and paperwork;

- is equipped in terms of Internet cables and power sockets so that you can use your phone and computer;

- is comfortable temperature-wise. You'll never get anything done if you're too cold or too hot – it's hard to concentrate on anything other than how uncomfortable you're feeling otherwise – so make sure the room has the right amount of heating and/or ventilation for you.

TOP TIP

Try, as far as you can, not to work in a dark room. While you can, obviously, boost the level of light with lamps, it can be very depressing to work in a dimly lit space, especially in the winter months. A brighter space, with plenty of natural light, will boost your spirits and keep you motivated. SAD lamps can be useful in the winter.

Step two: Make sure you're comfortable and that you have the right equipment

Office decor is important. It needs to be functional, but that doesn't mean it has to be boring or austere – you'll work much better in a room that you actually enjoy spending time in.

You don't have to spend a fortune, but choose good lighting, paint/wallpaper, floor covering and so on – or work in a room that has all of these already – so that your office is a good place to be.

Besides getting the right atmosphere, think about the communications side of things. If you are making a lot of video calls, is the backdrop of the room suitable for this? Is the Internet connection in the room you plan to use powerful enough? Even the best cable and fibre can run slowly in old buildings and if you are a long way from the router. Use a speedtest website to check and, if necessary, get an extender to make sure that your connection is both fast and stable enough in the room you plan to use. Remember that if someone else is also working from home, or using the Internet to do homework or stream, this will affect the speed of your connection.

Also, depending on how many screens and devices you will be using, check whether you need to run more electrical sockets into the room to support the equipment you need to use.

TOP TIP

If the business expects you to use a landline and you already have one at home, it might be worth investigating the cost of having a dedicated line installed. This will help keep work and home calls separate, which would be a big help if someone else is likely to be at home at the same time as you.

Your basic package of office equipment will depend on what industry you work in and what your level of activity is, but it will probably include:

- desk;

- chair;

- computer(s) and peripherals;

- software;

- landline, if required (see above);

- Internet connection;

- microphone and camera for video calls and meetings;

- a combined printer, scanner and copier (documents can be scanned on a mobile phone but, if you are required to scan multiple documents, a dedicated machine will be faster);

● filing cabinet;

● shredder, if you have confidential information and documents to dispose of.

If you're running your own business, you might want to invest in a really good camera set-up (e.g. lighting, tripod, reflectors) so that you can put photos of your products on a website. You can, of course, use your mobile phone for photos but a dedicated camera will give you more professional results. Depending on how often you need to take part in video calls and make presentations online, you might also consider buying equipment such as a ring light and good-quality wireless headphones to make sure you look as polished and professional as possible.

TOP TIP

If you're planning to use your home office for a small business, HMRC will allow you to deduct certain expenses connected to the business. Contact them to find out what they might be. Good record-keeping is very important if you plan to deduct expenses and part of the mortgage interest, utilities and phone bills for business activity. Visit HMRC's website for more information.

✔ Upgrade your connection to the Internet, if necessary. Use a speedtest website to determine how fast your current connection is and investigate whether a faster service would allow you to work more quickly and effectively, especially if other people are also working from home. If you're working for an employer, make sure you are up to date on their data security policies and able to access any information you may need via a VPN or remote server.

Finally, don't forget that you'll need some basic office supplies – pens, paper, Post-it notes, stapler, scissors, highlighter pens and so on.

TOP TIP

The sort of investment you'll need to kit out your home office will, of course, depend on the type of work you do. If you are working for a company from home full-time, they will usually provide you with a computer. If your work is hybrid (so half in the company office, half from home) you may be able to use your work laptop in both locations. If neither of these is the case, or your home computer is not fast enough, allow £1,000–£3,000. Make a list of what you need to use/do, including software and peripherals, and work out what you can afford. This is especially useful if you're starting your own business, as you don't want to blow your entire savings on setting up the office, and then have nothing to spend on attracting customers.

Step three: Think about ergonomics

Understand the benefits

Why do you need to bother with ergonomics? Because they're not a management fad, but a method of adapting equipment and surroundings so that you can work as efficiently as possible. The main aim is to create a safe, comfortable and stress-reduced environment, which sounds like just what you need when you're working from home.

In most workplaces, workstations are assessed to make sure that they are ergonomic and if you choose to work from home full- or part-time for a company, someone from your office may come and check whether your home working space conforms to the recommended standards. If not, it's worth making some checks for yourself. It may sound like one more thing to worry about that you just don't have time for, but it is worth being sensible – it will cut down on the risk of problems such as RSI and back ache for example. Some simple actions include:

✓ using a good-quality, adjustable chair to help avoid back problems;

✓ using an ergonomic mouse to reduce strain on the wrists and lower arm muscles;

✓ using a keyboard with palm rests.

Make yourself comfortable

Having a good chair is essential when you're spending a lot of time working at your desk. To make sure you're sitting comfortably:

✓ adjust the backrest and armrests of your chair so that you sit in an upright position and don't slouch. The backrest should follow the natural 'S' curve of your spine;

✓ lower or raise the height of the chair so that your wrists, hands and forearms are horizontal and level with the desk;

✔ place your feet flat on the floor or use a footrest if you prefer;

✔ keep your head up and your shoulders relaxed;

✔ remove any obstacles beneath your desk that prevent you from being able to fit your legs and feet underneath comfortably.

Watch out for eye strain

Many people get tired or sore eyes from working at their computer for much of the day. To help cut down on any discomfort:

✔ make sure your computer monitor is at a comfortable distance from your eyes;

✔ allow enough space on the desk to rest your hands and wrists, so that you can keep movement of the wrists to a minimum;

✔ adjust the brightness and colour contrast of your computer screen and make sure it is reflection-free and clean;

✔ avoid long periods of repetitive activity; for example, alternate computer-based work with other tasks, such as filing, calls or reading;

✔ if you spend a lot of time doing close work, such as checking contracts, make sure you have enough light to read by.

Keep it tidy!

When you choose a desk or recycle a table from elsewhere in the house to use as your desk, make sure it's big enough for you to work comfortably, as mentioned above, and also that it leaves you enough room to spread out the pieces of paper, books or other equipment that you need.

Whatever you do, try not to 'store' things on the floor; it's not only dangerous, but clutter will soon build up and make the office look like an uninviting bomb site. File things when you can and check through piles of paper regularly, being ruthless about what you can throw away, recycle or shred if appropriate.

TOP TIP

Don't worry too much about throwing away something important by accident. If the document really is that important, it will come back to you one way or another at a future date.

Step four: Think about insurance

Buildings and contents insurance

The majority of people who work from home tend to have reasonably sedentary desk-based tasks to do. If, however, your field of expertise or new business venture involves the manufacture or repair of goods, you should check that your existing buildings and contents insurance will cover your business activities too.

Computer insurance

Computer insurance may be worth investigating if you don't have it already. Some contents policies cover you for accidental damage and loss of information, but check that your cover includes cyber-attacks, damage to cables caused by rodents and power interruptions. Try to consider how much it would cost your business to be hacked for important data (both the loss and the PR damage can be costly) or to be forced offline for a few days and insure accordingly.

Step five: Check it all works!

Just think how frustrating it would be if, on your first day of working from home, nothing works: your computer won't boot up, you can't use your Internet and your mobile phone freezes.

To spare yourself all this stress, do a test run on a day agreed with your colleagues so that you can sort out any problems that arise well in advance. This will be particularly useful if you're working from home full-time or for a good proportion of the week. It will also give you a chance to set up a routine for your home working; see Chapter 3 for more information on this.

TOP TIP

If you rely on a computer when you're working at home, remember that you won't have the back-up systems in place that you have at the office. Most computers and software have automatic save functions built in but check that this is the case so that, if the worst comes to the worst and your computer crashes, you don't have to start everything from scratch. Working in/with cloud functions and cloud-based software will also help you, because they will save your documents/projects automatically and those documents are then accessible from every device you use.

Common mistakes

✗ You only go halfway

Starting a home office on the dining-room table isn't a good idea, and neither is committing only half-heartedly to making a guest room into a real office. If you don't treat the office seriously, there's a chance you won't take your work seriously, either. Carve out a separate space and dedicate it as the office; you'll feel better and your work will benefit from that decision.

BUSINESS ESSENTIALS

✓ Don't feel guilty about spending time planning the layout of your office; you'll be spending a lot of time there, so it's really important that you find a space that works for you.

✓ Make sure your office has plenty of natural light. Working in a dark space can be depressing and may have a negative impact on your mood and motivation, not to mention eye strain and poor visibility for video calls.

✓ Check that you have enough room in your office to work comfortably and to store all relevant paperwork and equipment.

✓ Think about the ergonomics of your office: is everything arranged so that it's functional but comfortable? If not, change it.

✔ Keep your office tidy! Don't use the floor as a storage space. It's not only dangerous to litter the floor with piles of paper or empty boxes, but you'll make the office a place that you don't want to visit. Check through all your paperwork regularly and recycle what you don't need.

✔ Make sure that you can contact people easily, and that they can contact you.

✔ Upgrade your Internet if needed/possible, and make sure you're up to date on data security.

✔ If you're working from home because you've set up a new business, work out a budget carefully and stick to it.

✔ Make sure your insurance is up-to-date and that it covers any new equipment you're using in your home office.

✔ Use automatic saving functions and/or cloud computing to make sure your work is safe and accessible from all devices.

✔ Do a test run before you launch yourself into your new working regime. This will let you iron out any problems or unforeseen hitches.

BUSINESS ESSENTIALS

3
Getting used to working from home

Working from home has become much more common over recent years, especially as technology has become more sophisticated and the pandemic made it more acceptable. But some people, especially those who have been used to working in larger companies, can take a while to get used to spending their office hours in a less structured setting. This chapter offers some advice on how to get the best from working at home and dodge some common issues.

Step one: Create some boundaries

As we said in Chapter 1, when you start working from home it's crucial that you set up a suitable work environment and set boundaries. It's hopeless trying to balance your laptop on your knee in the kitchen while you attempt to avoid intrusions from family or friends; you need to set rules for yourself and others so that everyone can support your efforts rather than sabotage them.

If there are other people at home, be clear about the time you set aside for working. Non-work interruptions can be frustrating when you're trying to get something done to a deadline.

✔ Establish in advance how you're going to manage your time at home, including things like the beginning and ending of your working day. Having a separate room to work in is key here as you can close the door and cut down on disturbances. Stick to your guns and people will soon get the message.

✔ If your work requires you to receive visitors, try to find an area where they won't be distracted by your domestic arrangements. Having to ignore the pile of washing on the kitchen floor can be very off-putting, however friendly you are with your guests. If you're unable to avoid these situations, find a local hotel or café where you can meet for an hour or two. Again, this is about creating boundaries that will enable you to maintain focus and create an impression of professionalism.

TOP TIP

If you're an extrovert and enjoy the buzz of having other people around, it's important to recognize and cater for this. You could try planning a certain number of days in the office and balance these with quieter, more productive days at home. If you're self-employed, you may need to schedule visits and meetings sufficiently regularly for you to feel involved with and energized by others.

Step two: Get into a routine

It's important to differentiate between being 'at work' and 'at home'. If your working and resting times become confused, it can feel as if you're always on duty, and when you do take a break you can feel guilty that you aren't finishing a project. This differentiation comes naturally when you have to travel to and from work, but when your routine changes you'll need to find a way to make this shift yourself. For example, it could be signalled by a routine: making a cup of coffee, taking it to your desk, closing your door and switching on the computer. Once you've done this a few times, this routine creates a boundary within which you can work effectively.

TOP TIP

Although the idea of wandering into your office pyjama-clad may appeal, get up and get dressed as if you were going into the office. Obviously you don't have to wear a suit or very smart clothes, but getting changed can be another effective 'signal' that you're starting your working day.

✓ Plan your day so that you don't find yourself wasting time. The advantage of working from home is that you have greater control over interruptions. People will no longer be able to wander past your desk at will and ask you for some information or, worse, to do something for them. A great deal of time is wasted in these 'Oh, by the way...' moments that happen mostly because you're accessible or visible.

Step three: Take regular breaks

✔ Make sure you take breaks throughout the day.
Most people's concentration starts to diminish after
about 20 minutes, and if you continue to work after
this time thinking can become a struggle. Taking a
break, perhaps a short walk, can re-energize your
thinking capability. Of course, breaks need to be
balanced by the need to be productive.

✔ Try not to get distracted by picking up something
else that needs doing. You'll only end up wasting
time and lowering your efficiency by spreading
your energies too thinly.

Step four: Work at your work–life balance

✔ Make sure you plan for the end of the day as well.

When you work at home, it's all too easy to stay sitting
in your workspace well into the evening and to ignore
the private side of your life. It can be hard to juggle
these two aspects of your life, but everyone needs a
break from work.

TOP TIP

Make some time for yourself, friends, family and other
interests; you'll be much happier in the long term.

Step five: Find out about your tax status

✔ If you are self-employed, having a home office
may qualify you for tax concessions. HMRC or an

accountant will guide you on what tax benefits you may receive. Anyone starting a new business must register with HMRC so visit their website for full information. You may also need to register for VAT too, depending on what your income will be. Find more information at www.gov.uk.

Common mistakes

✗ You lose your focus

For those who enjoy dynamic environments and the cut and thrust of being in a busy office, working from home may not be enjoyable. It's tempting for this type of person to create dynamism for themselves by finding activities that distract them from their own company. Flitting around from task to task can create a feeling of being 'in the flow', but may not be very productive. If you worry that you may be prone to finding 'displacement' activities rather than doing any work, spend a few minutes at the beginning of the day creating a to-do list. This will focus your energy and make sure that there's a valuable output to the day's activities.

✗ You can't switch off

It's very easy for people to work beyond the call of duty when the office is located in the home. This is especially the case if you've started a new business; the first stages can be really hectic and long hours are often unavoidable. 'I'll just go and answer a few emails...' can become a lengthy session in front of the computer or on your phone that eats into private time. Try to discipline yourself to keep to the 'rules' that you've set, with only occasional exceptions for real emergencies or key deadlines.

✗ You lose track of the time

If you miss the energy you get from working with others, you might turn to the phone as a substitute for their presence around you. It's easy to pass a lot of the day on the phone and to find that, as a result, you have to work late to actually achieve anything that day. Again, this is a question of discipline. Give yourself time to be in touch with others directly or on social media, but keep control of it. A large clock on the wall in front of you is a good reminder of how long you're spending on each activity!

BUSINESS ESSENTIALS

✓ Create some boundaries between your work space and your home space so that you can separate the two halves of your life more easily.

✓ Make some simple rules, such as having a clear start and end to the working day so that you and anyone who lives with you can get used to your new routine.

✓ Keep your work space tidy and welcoming so that any visitors to your home office won't be alarmed by your domestic arrangements!

✓ Plan your day so that you actually get something done. Make sure you also take regular breaks throughout the day, though, as they will help you keep your concentration levels up.

✓ Don't let yourself get distracted by household or garden chores that need doing. They can wait until you've got some work done.

✓ If you're an extrovert and benefit from having other people around, don't cut yourself off. Balance time in the office with quieter time at home so that you have the best of both worlds.

✓ Switch off in all senses at the end of the day. Keep to your rules and end your work day when you planned to.

Don't keep checking your email during the evening unless there's a genuine emergency or important deadline to deal with.

4
Learning to prioritize tasks

Keeping control of tasks is an essential skill to master, in any workplace and one that's particularly useful if you decide to work from home. Good prioritization helps you to avoid distraction and to become more efficient and self-reliant.

Some people naturally like structure in their life: control is one of the 'big five' personality factors that psychologists are able to agree on. If being in control is important to you and you enjoy structure, order and routines, it's unlikely that you'll struggle with the steps laid out below.

If, on the other hand, you prefer freedom and variety, you may feel constrained by structure and routines and find it harder to follow these steps. Persevere if you can, as you'll really reap some benefits. It might be a good idea to concentrate on using Step one, so that you're at least clear about what you're trying to achieve with your efforts. Learning to prioritize frees up a lot of time for whatever you would prefer to be doing. Use the steps below as a framework and schedule imaginatively, to give you the variety you need in your daily life.

Step one: Decide on your objectives

If you start off by being clear about what you want to achieve, the chances are that you'll succeed brilliantly. There are several levels to this step. Ask yourself:

- What do you (personally) want to get out of any particular period of work (say a month, six months)?

- What do your boss/team/clients/company need you to achieve during this time?

- What specific goals do you want to have achieved by the end of this month?

- ✓ Write the answers to these questions on a sheet of paper. Hang them in a prominent place in your office, ideally where a distracted eye will fall. You can add your objectives for your life outside work on an adjacent sheet of paper, if you feel inclined to do so.

You'll probably have several answers for each question, because our objectives are usually plural. If this is the case, you'll need to identify the relative importance of each element of your answer; it may help to organize your page with the most important elements first. Next to these will be the answers to the following questions, which it will become habitual to write at the beginning of the working week and day:

- What do you need to get done by the end of this week?

- What do you need to get done today?

The answers to these simple questions will guide
you through the chaos of each day. When faced with
requests or demands for your time and attention, ask
yourself how they'll help you towards your objectives:

- Should I do it now or after more important
  objectives have been met?
- Is this something I need to deal with today?
- Is this something I need to deal with this week?
- Do I need to sort it out this month?
- Can this go right on the end of my list, to do if I
  have time?
- Should I bother with this at all?
- Can I delegate this to someone else?

Step two: Use tools to help you

Although you don't want to clutter up your life even
further, there are some tools that can help you live
according to your priorities.

Diary

A diary helps you to plan ahead, appropriately
scheduling specific dates or times for tasks and
actions. It helps you to structure time towards
deadlines so that you can monitor interim goals more
easily and make sure they're met, with your ultimate
goal being to deliver the outcome you want on time.

✔️ Divide projects and objectives into constituent parts and place 'milestones' in your diary. Don't forget to schedule time to meet people, or you could risk isolating yourself.

A diary is especially useful to structure your time if you have lots of short meetings or telephone calls or if you need long chunks of time to focus on difficult, complex or creative work. By communicating your need to your colleagues and concentrating meetings and other work into one section of the day or week, you free yourself to work in a more effective manner.

Diaries come in multiple formats. While computer or phone formats may offer useful features, a paper diary also does the job just as well. Choose whichever one works best for you.

To-do list

In its simplest form, a to-do list is a place to record the things you need to do, so that you can tick them off as you achieve them. Apps on phones and on your computer may offer extra features but, again, a simple paper list is fine.

If you're aware that you take on too many tasks, a to-do list may help you to visualize your workload and manage requests more assertively. Always keep your objectives in mind when you're writing your to-do list.

✔️ Next to each entry on your list give the task a number to reflect the priority of the task relative to your objectives and the other tasks. You can even make your list public so that your boss and colleagues can see the work already assigned and do some of the prioritizing for you.

Time audit

This is a backwards look at how you've been spending your time. It's a useful tool to monitor how well you're focusing your time on the objectives you want to achieve, and where things have gone awry.

✔ Looking back through your diary and to-do list, estimate the amount of time that you spent working towards the objectives you set yourself. Do the same for your time and objectives outside work. How does your time allocation tally? What needs to change in the future: your objectives and priorities or your time management?

Project planner

When managing projects, a project planning system can help you to break down a complex system easily into its constituent elements, identify milestones, assign tasks to others and keep track of progress. This can be done on paper, on a whiteboard or flipcharts or on your computer and/or phone.

> **TOP TIP**
>
> 'Prioritize' is a verb. That means action, not tools. People can have a very fancy toolkit to help them but it has no effect until they use it. Don't fool yourself that having a diary and a to-do list means that you're organized. Even filling them in will not help alone. It's the discipline of following the schedule in your diary and focusing on the completion of each task on the to-do list that will make you efficient and successful.

Step three: Manage your inputs and outputs

The process of working efficiently comes in managing the inputs as they happen and remaining focused on the output of the most important and urgent task.

First and most important: be clear which set of objectives you should be focused upon now – work or home objectives. If you work from home, separate your work space from your home space as far as you can. Separate work time from home time, work phone from home phone, and home email from work email too. This way, you can protect yourself from the stress of role confusion.

Managing output

It's a good idea to write a checklist of things to do when you start your work time.

- Look up at your objectives on the wall to focus on what you're achieving.

- Look at your diary and see what you've scheduled and how much time you have spare.

- Look at your to-do list and pick out the tasks that are the most important and urgent. You can choose to start a long task and finish it on a different day or you may prefer to pick a single task that will fit within the time you have available.

- Allow yourself time for interruptions and three or four 10-minute breaks and a longer meal break within a working day. You'll be more focused and effective if you stay fresh. Now you can write your objectives for the day.

Managing input

✓ Make your days more efficient by allocating time slots to emails and phone calls.

✓ How you do this will depend on your role, but for most people physical post will only need attention once a day. Emails, however, may take more time. Sort them both as follows. Divide incoming messages into:

● junk: straight into the bin;

● items to file for reference;

● items to deal with immediately: respond to each one quickly and efficiently;

● items requiring more attention: add to your to-do list or schedule specific time in your diary. Don't forget to think about how important the item is to the achievement of your objectives.

Emails carry the expectation that they'll be seen and dealt with immediately and some may generate more interruptions if left too long. On the other hand, very few roles require that people need to respond to each email as it arrives. Allocate a maximum of three slots in the day for responding to email. Start the day with a quick check, check again after lunch and do a final check as you finish work for the day.

TOP TIP

Turn off notifcations on your desktop and phone as they will distract you if they make a noise each time you get a new message.

How you deal with your phones depends on your role. You may be expected to answer calls immediately during office hours. Perhaps you prefer to have the variety of contact with others throughout the day and enjoy the social side of the interruption. Some calls may be quickly dealt with if answered immediately, saving yourself and others time.

✓ If your role allows it, try to switch on voicemail and return calls during allocated slots through the day, as with emails. If this system is compatible with your role, it will allow you greater focus on your objectives for the day, making you more productive. But it does require you to get into the habit of regularly checking and returning calls.

TOP TIP

Whatever your line of work, try not to put off 'horrible' jobs. They'll have to be done at some point, and it's a good idea to tackle them early in the day. That way, you'll feel as if you've accomplished something within just a short time of starting work and you'll also be able to concentrate better on other tasks, as you'll no longer be worrying about the job you'd been dreading.

Common mistakes

✗ You confuse housework with work

Part of the beauty of working from home may be the flexibility. But don't fool yourself that you're working if you are in fact fixing things around the house or doing the washing. Restrict these activities to before work, after work or during a lunch break.

✗ Your standards drop over time

You owe it to yourself to put in a full and focused day towards your objectives or it's unlikely that you'll meet them. If it helps, imagine your boss or colleague's reaction to a piece of work you're finishing. Does it do you justice?

BUSINESS ESSENTIALS

✔ Know what you're trying to achieve. Bringing abstract, large or vague objectives into current targets by breaking them down into smaller and more manageable chunks makes them more achievable. If you have trouble doing this, get help from your boss or a business coach.

✔ Keep the correct set of objectives in mind at all times and stay focused.

✔ Know your tools and how to use them. If in doubt about the technology, work a dual-system approach until you're certain that you can rely upon it.

✔ Build your own way of managing inputs and outputs based upon the suggestions in this section into your routine. Have a schedule that helps you and stick to it.

✔ Be clear about your different roles and try to keep them separate. There will be times when you're required to switch between them but don't allow this to become routine.

✔ If you find you're slipping back into your old haphazard methods, return to this section regularly to remind yourself. If you struggle at first, have faith! Anyone can learn to prioritize but it may take some time for it to become habitual.

5
Maintaining your relationships with the office and key contacts

Why is the maintenance of a working network so important? Because whether you're working alone at home or in a busy office, you'll need a network around you to get things done. It's also easy to feel isolated if you don't maintain regular contact with others, as we'll see in Chapter 7.

Remember that:

- your network may offer inputs: by gathering, processing and passing on information to you; by procuring services or items required for your work; by sharing insight, ideas, opportunities and expertise with you;

- your network may also provide outputs: by doing work that you delegate; by passing on information to others; by making decisions that help you to proceed effectively;

● when you're working at home you're all the more likely to need a strong network to be as effective as you can in your work. If you spend time looking after your work relationships, you'll be protecting yourself against some of the downsides of being out of the office for some or all of the week.

Step one: Think about your current key contacts

Take a clean sheet of paper and draw a mind map to identify the main groups of key contacts that you maintain in order to perform your everyday work.

For example:

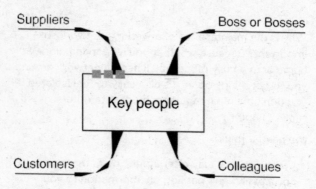

Step two: Think about who your future key contacts might be

Now, using a different colour, identify the kind of contacts that could be helpful to you in the future. The idea is to list groups with the potential to help, rather than just those you are sure will help you. As you can see below, the number of branches on the map quickly increases and this is before you've even started to list the various individuals under each branch.

For example:

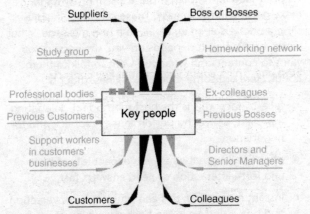

The network represented by the black arrows represents your main contact group and the people with whom you're in most regular contact. The network represented by the grey arrows is the one that you need to build.

> **TOP TIP**
>
> It's best to create and work at building your network before you need it to help you out. Well-connected people often seem to be more 'lucky' than others are; they frequently seem to be in the right place at the right time. In fact, what they've done is to work hard at making those connections that could lead to the big assignment, important new customer or dream job they've been looking for.

Step three: Keep in touch!

Think about the best way to do it.

As discussed in Chapter 2, there are many ways to make getting in touch easy. These can range from a simple phone call, to an email, to a text message. What works best? Well, it depends on you, the person you want to contact, and what you want to talk to them about. Here are some rough guidelines, though:

- face-to-face: this is the best method for delegating a project, delivering performance feedback and for negotiation;

- phone calls: great when you expect lots of back and forth interaction or need answers fast;

- instant messaging: this can simulate a conversation and be carried on in the background, much in the same way that office chat takes place in an open-plan environment;

- email: good for collaboration on attached files, nice when you want to refer to a record of your 'conversation' and very useful for global interactions, where time differences make phone contact difficult.

Think about when and how often to contact others

Your current network is clearly a priority and you'll have the details of those people close to hand, so it's a good idea to start there. For each person, you need to decide what you're going to do to maintain the relationship and how frequently, but it's a good idea to follow this general pattern:

- make contact;
- keep it genuine;

✓ keep it short;

✓ make it a habit.

Keeping in contact isn't supposed to be a chore, so as well as phone calls or online chats, take a break from the same-old same-old and think about meeting for:

● breakfast;

● coffee;

● lunch or dinner;

● drinks at a pub or bar;

● a day out at a sporting event;

● a visit to a theatre or show.

TOP TIP

Maintain your relationships carefully and don't be selfish. If you only contact people when you want something, you'll create an 'uh-oh' effect when you call. Relationships need oiling in-between times to ensure they are ready, rather than rusty, when you need them. Always ask others if there's anything you can do to help them. The easiest relationships to maintain are those that are based upon genuine and comfortable interactions between individuals.

✓ Try to identify ways of making the other person feel comfortable and confident when they talk to you. This doesn't mean using the shallow compliments of sales patter. Learning and paying attention to what is important to the other will make a big difference to the relationship that you build.

With the contacts that you have already, you'll have to make greater effort to make sure that the rapport you've already built doesn't fade. Now that you're out-of-sight in your home office, this means short but regular contact, with occasional face-to-face contact when you can. Make a point of attending office socials, such as launch events, Christmas parties, team lunches or drinks.

With new contacts, actively building the relationship with people is critical. Although it may seem obvious, this is where people often fall down when they're trying to increase their network – if you meet a new contact, swap business cards and never do anything about it, your network will never grow. Be proactive instead. Contact people after a few days with a simple note or email and then arrange to meet up after a month or so – you'll be much more likely to develop a relationship from the initial meeting.

TOP TIP

If you decide to phone someone to keep up your contact, it's really useful to be able to refer to what you've said in previous conversations. Being able to refer to the content of your previous calls is a great help here. Taking notes after each contact to jog your memory later will help to create trust and rapport between you and your contact and give an excellent impression.

Common mistakes

✗ You rely on too few contacts

Reliance on too few contacts may mean that they become exhausted. Make sure that you spread requests for help and that you make the interaction truly two-way.

✗ You deluge your contacts with junk mail

If the only contact you have with someone is the jokes you send them by email, you have no relationship at all. When you finally try to contact them for real, you may find that they've banned contact from your email address to reduce the junk in their mailbox.

BUSINESS ESSENTIALS

✓ Whether you work from home or from the office, your working network is crucial. It will, in very basic terms, help you do your job better.

✓ Take the initiative in keeping up contact with others if you work from home.

✓ Start by identifying which people currently enable you to get things done, as they're the people you really need to be in touch with.

✓ Think about where your network could be stronger and start making contacts. The better connected you are, the 'luckier' you'll become!

✔ Find a way to keep in contact that fits with your style and suits who you're talking to and what you want to say. Be imaginative!

✔ Use your diary to remind yourself to get in touch with those whom you don't work with regularly. Keep the network fresh for when you really need it.

6
Working as part of a virtual team

Working as part of a virtual team is obviously something you will experience if you work from home.

In very broad strokes, a virtual team is a group of people who use technology to collaborate from different bases. Members of a virtual team may all work for the same company, be a mix of employees and freelancers, or be entirely freelance. Team members may be scattered across one country or all around the world.

Virtual teams were becoming commonplace before the COVID-19 pandemic, as businesses opened up offices around the world to expand their reach, but since 2020 they have become an essential and economical way of collaborating.

However, although working virtually helps keep time and cost investments to a minimum, it does mean colleagues and team members remain physically isolated from each other. Although technology is an incredible tool, it is a poor substitute for the chemistry that teams create as they work together face-to-face, getting the best from each person's strengths and characteristics. So, knowing how to build a successful virtual team is a valuable skill, and one that can add positive aspects to your decision to work from home.

Step one: Think about the qualities needed for an effective virtual team

An effective virtual team has the same qualities as a team working in close proximity. Good virtual team members are:

- collaborative in their work. They share information, knowledge, ideas, views and experiences in order for the team to pull together as a unit;

- trusting of each other. Each member needs to know that the others will meet their promises promptly without personal agendas getting in the way;

- attentive to communication. Each member has to agree priorities and communicate progress regularly. There should be no withholding of information. Good communication only happens when every member takes responsibility for being part of the team and is committed to the team's overall purpose;

- skilled at building relationships. In the absence of actual face-to-face meetings, the development of strong, trusting relationships will depend even more than usual upon excellent communication;

- agreed on how they'll work together. All team members should agree on ground rules, written down or not, governing how they operate.

Step two: 'Meet' all members of the team and get to know something about them

Before you start to work as part of a virtual team, it's a good idea to get in touch with your colleagues and get to know them a bit better. Phone or video-call them if you can, and if time zones allow. We're all aware of the hazards of communicating by email (such as your tone being misinterpreted, irony not always travelling very well, and so on), whereas a conversation will help to get a feel of what your colleagues are like in 'real life'.

✓ Look for similarities of values, interests, expertise or experience so that you have a bridge into the relationship. Building rapport is the first step to being part of an effective team; without this, there's nothing to cement the team together.

If you're about to take responsibility for managing a virtual team, you won't be able to move through traditional team-building phases and will need to think of a back-up plan.

✓ Try setting up an extensive briefing session via video or a training programme that encourages information-sharing and collaboration. In this way, you'll put team members in a position where they have to build good communication channels and trust among themselves.

TOP TIP

Obviously it's much easier to build trust and rapport when you can actually see someone and communicate spontaneously. You only need do this once or twice to kick-start your relationship. For this reason, it's worth having one video call with those members of your team who live in compatible time zones and a second with those who couldn't join you on the first call. Encourage the others to do the same, passing real-time communication around the team like the baton in a relay race. In this way, even though you can't meet everyone at the same time, you can still meet each member face-to-face.

Step three: Agree and assign the different roles in the team

✓ As a group, decide who plays which part in assisting the team to meet its objectives. Work out the resources and support that you'll need in order to play your part effectively. This exercise demands that everyone is honest: it's great to share talents and strengths, but you also need to be aware of knowledge gaps so that you can plug them.

✓ Set boundaries around tasks and agree timescales. Decide collectively how the team will deal with failures to meet its objectives. You may sometimes need to call emergency meetings to create contingency plans, set new timescales or realign the team's objectives.

✓ Agree how regularly you'll check in with each other. These reviews are designed primarily to make sure that all projects are on track, but they'll also act as early-warning systems if something is beginning to go wrong. These sessions are really important, so everyone needs to be committed to taking part in them.

✓ Discuss the possibility of conflict and decide how you'll deal with this. Many people hate even the thought of conflict and tend to ignore the possibility until it actually emerges and needs to be dealt with. Conflict isn't always a negative experience; if it's handled well and sensitively, it can clear the air and be positive in the long run.

Step four: Make technology work for you

There are so many different options and technologies that will help your virtual team work better. Take time to think about which one will be most suitable for which working practice. Here are some examples:

- video calls and presentations. Best suited to meeting with lots of participants and for detailed information sharing;

- collaboration software and storage (e.g. via Dropbox, Huddle, Trello). This software enables team members to manage projects, organize tasks and share documents;

- using group email. The ability to send email to one or every member of the team greatly enhances the team's ability to communicate but be wary of using it in a kneejerk fashion. Ask yourself if everyone needs to be on the email, or if a more targeted list would be more productive;

- message boards. Message or bulletin boards enable group members to go to a central place where communication can take place and information is stored and is readily accessible;

- online communication tools. Applications such as Microsoft Teams and Slack offer instant messaging among individuals and groups, dedicated channels for specific topics of conversation, and spaces to store files and host meetings.

Step five: Celebrate success

It's all too easy for dispersed teams to forget to celebrate their achievements, but it's important to mark the attainment of goals. Celebration allows you to release tension, enjoy your success and move on to the next challenge.

✔ Organize a video call to celebrate, not just collaborate. Although this may feel a little contrived, it nonetheless allows a form of togetherness and mutual appreciation. It also invites humour as you review what went well and what didn't, so it's a great way of letting things go and getting them into perspective.

Step six: Learn from the experience

T.S. Eliot wrote: 'It is possible to have the experience yet miss the meaning.' If you don't learn, you don't develop and grow. Take time to reflect on how you took your part in the team and what you've learned about yourself from doing so. What would you do differently or better next time?

Common mistakes

✗ You don't build up rapport and trust

Not spending enough time on building rapport and trust will sabotage any team, but it's a definite no-no when working online and remotely. It's easy to assume that everyone has the same high level of commitment to the team's formation and purpose as the co-ordinator or leader, but if you're in charge you need to check that everyone does feel like that. If you're a team member, you need the chance to tell someone if you're worried about or disheartened by something. Give team members an opportunity to get to know each other so that they can work out how their talents and skills will work together to reach your collective objectives. This means either a physical team-building meeting or a series of virtual gatherings.

✗ You communicate badly

Forgetting to communicate with colleagues is one of the main reasons that virtual teams fail. In the absence of physical proximity and the ability to pass quick messages or information over a cup of coffee in the office, out of sight can quickly become out of mind. Be sure to schedule regular meetings – and hold them without fail.

✗ You don't establish clear understanding of roles and expectations

It's important that all members understand both their role in the team and the expectations that the team leader and the members have of each other. It's too easy to assume that this is obvious. If you're the leader, you need to be crystal-clear about this from the outset or the team will disintegrate into conflict.

BUSINESS ESSENTIALS

✓ Spend time getting to know your virtual colleagues, and schedule regular video calls so that the team can meet 'face-to-face'. It's much easier to build relationships when you can all see each other – even if it is on screen.

✓ Make the most of technology to help your team collaborate effectively. Whether this means an instant messaging programme or collaboration software like Trello or Huddle, your team will work better if everyone is able to easily ask questions and share resources.

✓ Make time for the occasional virtual social event, such as an after-work 'happy hour' or an informal video call over lunch. Socializing as a group helps with team bonding, and it's always good to come together to celebrate a success.

✓ Be mindful of any differences in time zones, and make sure meetings are scheduled at a time that's appropriate for everyone.

7
Coping with feelings of isolation

When people switch from working in an office to working from home, they often find that they miss the social side of working life. The natural contacts of the daily commute, bumping into friends in the kitchen and the general banter of office life, lunches or after-work activities may be things you're happy to give up in practice, but how will you cope with the reality of working from home?

Step one: Keep in contact with others

Even if you're someone who generally likes their own company, it can be lonely to spend a lot of the day or the week on your own. It's important to keep in touch with colleagues when you work from home for all sorts of reasons, but even more so if you get a boost from being in touch with others. The key here is ease of connection.

✓ Start by making sure people can contact you easily when they want to. And be happy to hear from them! The easier it is to contact you, the more likely people are to take the trouble to get in touch and keep in touch.

> **TOP TIP**
>
> Make some noise! For some people, lack of noise in their environment is a constant reminder that they are alone. If you're not enjoying birdsong from the garden and find the silence a little too deafening, putting on some low-key music or turning on the radio for background noise can be a good addition to your home office.

Step two: Make the most of 'socials'

Even though you may have moved out of an office environment, it's a good idea to attend relevant in-person training sessions to boost your skills or just keep in the loop.

Similarly, if your employing organization is in a state of flux, make sure you attend meetings about major changes that are taking place so that you're in touch with your colleagues and they remember that you're affected by potential rejigging too.

Keeping in touch doesn't have to be a chore, and social events are a great way of staying visible.

✔ Go to all events you're invited to, such as the Christmas party, product launches and leaving dos. At these events in particular, you have a perfect opportunity to introduce yourself to new members of the team in a relaxed situation. This will mean

that staff turnover doesn't contribute to any
feelings of isolation you may have.

✓ Take responsibility for staying in contact
in-between social events and always think of
the ball as being in your court.

Step three: Make regular contact with support workers

When you work under pressure in an office
environment, there are usually people around you
who can sympathize or spread the load. Delegating
even small parts of a task not only makes a physical
impression on the work to be done, but also has a
positive psychological effect and can therefore reduce
the burden considerably. When you come under
pressure in your home office, there's a distance barrier
between you and your support system, and this is
when feelings of isolation are most likely to kick in.

Regardless of the type of work that you do, there are
usually some particular people whom you rely on or
work closely with.

✓ Be friendly with your team and colleagues in
regular, positive but brief phone calls or emails. Ask
light, open questions such as 'what's new?' that will
prompt them to update you with all the gossip and
changes afoot. Remember that you need to give
something back, so encourage them to share their
ups and downs with you and offer support and
laughs in return.

Keeping in touch like this helps you in two ways: you
learn what's going on in the office and you keep your
office-based colleagues on-side and friendly, which will

be important when you need their help. If you've got into the habit of having these 'chats' and supporting others by phone, you will feel less alone when you are the one needing help or a friendly ear.

Step four: Join or start a local group for people in the same boat

This one isn't for everyone but joining or setting up a group of like-minded home-workers or a professional group with interests in your field could be just the source of contacts you need to avoid isolation.

✓ Meet for breakfast, lunch, dinner or drinks and get to know members personally as well as at a professional level. If you offer support to others, they are likely to reciprocate when your spirits are in need of a lift. These environments will also help you to build your network and can be very constructive for your career.

TOP TIP

Don't put yourself under extra pressure by thinking you're the only home-worker who feels isolated. Compared with the busy office environment you're used to, you're bound to feel alone at times in your new work environment. If it gets too much, take your laptop out to lunch or for a coffee! The change of scene will do you good; just being in a restaurant or café environment with people around you making a bit of noise and bustle can be enough to make the difference to your mood.

Step six: Remember you're not super-human

Some people are very resourceful and self-reliant in their working style, preferring to carry out their work alone and solve their problems by themselves. If this sounds like you, you may also recognize the tendency to shoulder all the pressure and 'be strong'. Toughing out busy periods in this way can put a lot of stress on your system, so confide in people you trust and admit it if you need help – this isn't a sign of weakness. No one can be strong all the time and if you don't allow others to help you, you're adding unnecessary pressure to your load.

TOP TIP

Slot in a regular sanity check by setting aside some time each week when you stop to consider how you're feeling. Having some time out to think about yourself, rather than all your other tasks, will help you take action to get the contact you need before feelings of slight loneliness turn into more serious isolation blues.

Common mistakes

✗ You bombard your partner with questions

If you work at home and your partner or housemate works in a busy environment, you may recognize this scenario. You've spent the day closeted away, without anyone to share your thoughts, and could really use a good chat. But what if your partner is feeling drained by the constant distractions or demands of others in their work environment and just wants to be left alone? Your needs at the end of the day are likely to be quite different, so be sensitive and give the other person some time and space where it's required.

✗ You go too far the other way

Having encouraged visitors to drop by to stave off isolation, you may find that once people know you're at home they turn up too often and stay for too long. The best solution, as you can imagine, is all about balance: for productivity's sake you may need to set a few parameters to manage this type of distraction without discouraging it completely.

✗ You have too many 'virtual' contacts

The Internet can be great for making contact with others in your field or other home-workers, but this level of interaction will never replace real one-to-one human communication. Even if you're pushed for time, it's well worth making the effort to talk to people face-to-face regularly.

BUSINESS ESSENTIALS

✓ Before you take the plunge of working from home full-time, think about whether you're naturally suited to it or whether you're likely to find it lonely and tough. If you do go ahead, make some plans about how you'll get enough contact with other people to keep you happy.

✓ Make sure that you have the tools of your trade set up from day one. The first few weeks can be very demanding after you change your work environment, and you may feel the need to prove yourself as a successful home-worker. You don't need to be coping with technology teething problems on top of all this pressure.

✓ Home-working doesn't necessarily mean that you never visit your colleagues or see the whites of your boss's eyes! You can still attend important meetings, training and social events.

✓ Make sure that you keep on top of changes back at the office by your informal contact with colleagues and support workers. The onus will be on you to make contact and ask questions. You don't need to be heavy-handed about this; a simple email or phone call to say hello, and to ask how things are, is all you need.

✓ Make new contacts in your local area so that you don't rely too heavily on calls to your work colleagues for support. The advantages are that you will increase your network at the same time as getting the face-to-face contact you require.

✓ Create a backdrop of (appropriate!) noise if you find silence oppressive. Having music blaring out might not be the best idea (especially if you find yourself scrabbling to find the 'off' button on your stereo when your boss rings you unexpectedly), but low-key music or talk radio will help you feel as if you're not completely on your own.

✔ Don't let 'being strong' become your Achilles' heel; you're only human and there's only so much you can take on and do well. Ask for help if you need it rather than struggling on.

8
Setting up as a free agent

As mentioned back in Chapter 1, many people are seduced by the idea of commuting in dressing gown and slippers to an office only a few yards away from the breakfast table. The next logical step for some people is to leave their current position to start their own business.

Could you cut the mustard? To start, ask yourself the following questions:

- How much of my freelance fantasy is based on being unhappy with my current situation?

- What is my 'core competency', around which I will begin a freelance business?

- Who employs freelancers in my field of work and do I have enough experience and contacts?

- Who is my competition and what edge do I have over them?

- What are the costs of going into my own business, as well as the benefits?

Step one: Think about what being a freelancer really means

The word 'freelance' comes from the old days of knights-for-hire, but these days it refers to someone working, or available to work, for more than one employer for agreed lengths of time. Nowadays, a freelancer can be a self-employed person in any number of industries, including accounting, writing, film and video, management consulting, software development and Internet services.

What sort of personality traits and skills must a person have as a freelancer?

You must be – or quickly become – confident, resourceful, enterprising, adventurous, flexible and organized. As a business owner, you also must be a manager, a book-keeper and a promoter. You'll have to be able to 'multi-task' – juggle a number of diverse projects, each with different deadlines, for your clients. Finally, you'll need to get used to not only a different way of working, but to being the person with whom the buck stops in all work matters.

How do I decide what to charge for my services?

There are books and websites that give guidelines about the value of your profession, in terms of an hourly rate. Another way to determine your fees is to work out what people in your field earn per hour as employees, then add 25–50 per cent to account for the overheads you'll have (such as taxes, retirement savings, insurance, equipment and supplies).

If possible, find out what established freelancers in your field are charging. You may want to start at a reduced rate for the first year, especially if you're going to be competing for work against those with more experience.

Remember, too, that as a business owner, at least a quarter of your workload will involve activities you may not invoice for, such as research, marketing, promotion and bookkeeping.

TOP TIP

Some people have found it a good idea to start a freelance business on a part-time basis, so that they can still rely on the income from their other job during the tricky start-up phase. This part-time approach may take on the dimensions of a second full-time job and as a result cut into other areas of your life, but trying it out this way will show you quickly if you have the determination and work ethic to persevere.

Step two: Do your research

Making a jump to freelancing requires a kind of 'inside-out' approach.

✔ Be honest with yourself about your motives for the move. If you feel more excitement about the future than dread about your current position, you're on the right track.

✓ Look at your personality assets: you'll need people skills, energy, promotional creativity, a love of your chosen profession and a devotion to detail. Your outside research should include canvassing the industry in which you'll offer your services.

✓ Determine how big a 'territory' you'll initially serve, and what sort of companies. If possible, ask the advice of anyone already in that field. In the best of all worlds, knowing someone at those companies who knows you from a prior work relationship (and who can therefore recommend you) is a big asset.

Step three: Develop your business plan

Once you decide to commit to a life as a freelancer – but before you leave your day job – write a business plan. Even if you've already lined up a client or two, a business plan will plot the first year's goals and activity.

Not only will your business plan help you clarify your business's purpose and prepare well for the future, it's also essential if you want to borrow money from the bank or another financial institution. You need to convince other people to be as committed to the business as you are, so remember to:

✓ be as specific as possible about the kind of business you're starting;

✓ describe your business in terms of a mission statement or 'executive summary' that clearly summarizes your business's purpose;

✓ make sure your purpose can be easily understood by you, your customers and potential investors. If you can't describe your business in this way, you really need to go back and rethink your business idea and focus on the core activities and direction;

✓ remember that creating a business plan will help you as well as investors – it will help you focus.

TOP TIP

Use your vision of where you want your business to be in five years as a starting point. Then show in your business plan how you will move towards that point. For example, you might work towards becoming a market leader, an innovator, a specialist, a large concern or a top-notch supplier.

Step three: Market and promote your business

Whether or not your freelance business is in the same industry you're currently employed in, you'll need to develop a target list of companies that you'd like to work for. Once you've done that:

✓ learn all you can about each company, its products and services, its financial health, its challenges and its history with contract/freelance employees. Find out who in those companies makes decisions to employ freelancers. Aim your marketing and proposals at them; invite them to lunch if they happen to live nearby.

Marketing can also include letters, brochures or emails sent to potential customers, as well as personal networking, advertising and promotional activities, even a website. Hopefully, you'll have built enough of a network before you start your business to reduce the amount of 'cold calling' you must do.

Step four: Focus on customer service

Making the move to being a profitable freelancer is largely a matter of time: the longer you're in business, the greater the probability that you'll be successful. Remember that it's far better to keep a current client happy than to spend the same amount of time finding another one, so being prompt and delivering a professional product or service for the proposed budget are the cornerstones of a successful freelance business.

> **TOP TIP**
>
> Don't underestimate the value of being liked!
>
> Having a good personal manner and being a great communicator often makes up for the few flaws the client may eventually find in your work.

Step five: Keep up good business practices and stay organized

As a freelancer, it would be rare to have a consistent client, or set of clients, for a long period of time. Business climates change, and freelancers are vulnerable to shifts in policy and personnel: if your in-house contact moves on, for example, the new person may have their own preferred freelancers, so you may lose out. Having said that, always keep on good terms with your contacts, so that they'll want you to 'move' with them when the time comes!

✔ Get used to the idea of losing clients and gaining new ones; it's part of the nature of the business, like an animal shedding a winter coat and growing a new one.

To protect themselves against this inevitability, freelancers usually have several irons in the fire. It often takes six months to a year to secure work with a new prospective client.

✔ Discipline yourself to plan at least six months ahead to ensure a steady stream of work.

Learn to anticipate when clients need more service, but also learn to predict when your tenure may be drawing to a close. Have the foresight to build enough diversity in your client base that the loss of one won't spell disaster for your business.

Common mistakes

✗ You're cavalier about your home office

Many freelancers begin at home and there's nothing wrong with that. But be very careful (for HMRC purposes) to keep good records of allowable expenses. HMRC has specific guidelines under which you may deduct expenses and it is important to pay attention to them.

✗ You rely too much on one client

In the best sense, contractors and freelancers bring added value to a company, and companies are willing to pay handsomely for those who can deliver. But don't become complacent – valued as you may feel, contractors are easier to lay off than employees, so when it comes to budget-tightening or changes in administrative personnel be vigilant and prepared. While having a contract may give you some security, it isn't a guarantee.

For this reason, freelance work is often more volatile than being an employee, and the best advice is to insulate yourself against leaner times by having a variety of clients. HMRC also takes a dim view of contractors only working for one client and, if it can be proved that you should in fact be classified as an employee and not a freelancer, then you and your employer may be subject to fines for underpayment of tax.

✗ You don't save for the lean times

Inevitably, there will be times in your freelance business when you have less work. Putting aside enough money to get you through, say, two or three months of basic expenses is advisable. Besides that, however, remember that as a freelancer, you're also responsible for paying taxes to HMRC. Make sure you're aware of what these are likely to be and create a reserve in readiness for this. However, don't forget to pay yourself, including salary and appropriate provision for your retirement. Try to save for holidays too; we all benefit from a break.

X You let things slide

Just as you must be adept and professional about what you bill your client for, you also must become skilled at running your own business affairs. Plan to devote up to 25 per cent of your time to various administrative and marketing-related activities. When business is booming, it's especially easy to get complacent about record-keeping, credit card debt, payment of taxes, developing new business leads and even collecting from your clients on time. If you don't stay on top of your own business details, you could be ruined very quickly when times are harder.

For tax purposes and others, it's well worth hiring an accountant. They can tell you how to avoid tax troubles and they'll often save you more in deductions than you'll pay them in fees. They have lots of experience advising business people about a variety of issues, so feel free to ask them for information. If they're reluctant to advise you, ask around and find another one.

BUSINESS ESSENTIALS

✓ Think about whether you have the right personality to work for yourself. A short commute may seem like a benefit but there are lots of other things to consider, such as whether you are happy working alone and being responsible for all the decision-making in every aspect of the business.

✓ Do some research into your market and your competition, to determine your company's USP and what you can offer and charge.

✓ Write a detailed business plan outlining the specifics of what you hope to achieve and by when. This will help you focus and can also be used as a document for investors.

✓ Allow time, money and energy for marketing. It's all very well doing a good job, but if it's the last job you do because nobody has heard of you, that isn't very productive. It is essential for tax purposes to have more than one client so allow time to find new ones.

✓ Offer great customer service and don't be afraid to be liked. Clients like to work with people they get on with, to know that a job will be done to the highest standards and that any problems will be dealt with speedily and efficiently. The easier and cheerier you are to work with and solve problems, the more work you will get.

✓ Stay organized. Plan your workload and your finances so you can always work efficiently and deal with unexpected issues.

Where to find more help

Working from Home: Making the New Normal Work for You

Karen Mangia

London: Wiley, 2020

192pp

ISBN: 978-1119758921

Published in the year of the COVID-19 pandemic, this book is a strategic and practical guide to working remotely all the time. The author, a Salesforce expert, shows you how to have a successful career even without being in the office.

HBR Guide to Remote Work

Cambridge, Mass.: Harvard Business Review Press, 2021

240pp

ISBN: 978-1647820527

A home-working guide from the respected *Harvard Business Review* that outlines how to make working at home a success for you.

Remote Not Distant: Design a Company Culture That Will Help You Thrive in a Hybrid Workplace

Gustavo Razzetti

Chicago: Liberationist Press, 2022

326pp

ISBN: 978-0999097397

A guide for leaders and company owners, this book aims to focus on the practices and approaches that will enable businesses to gain from remote working, now that it is an established practice.

Going Remote: How the Flexible Work Economy Can Improve Our Lives and Our Cities

Matthew E. Kahn

Berkeley: University of California Press, 2022

282pp

ISBN: 978-0520384316

For those who want to think about what home-working means, from a wider perspective, this is an excellent analysis and evaluation from a leading urban economist.

www.gov.uk

For essential UK information on tax and allowable expenses as a freelancer.

Index

BUSINESS ESSENTIALS